SHOW ME HOW FAST IT IS!

by **Jerry Pallotta**

Illustrated by **Rob Bolster**

SCHOLASTIC INC.

New York   Toronto   London   Auckland   Sydney
Mexico City   New Delhi   Hong Kong   Buenos Aires

To Marsha Grace, Mary Beth Tierce, and
Tina Ybarra   —J.P.

To the Lund family and their incredible wit
                                     —R.B.

ISBN-13: 978-0-545-08582-3
ISBN-10: 0-545-08582-9

Text copyright © 2008 by Jerry Pallotta
Illustrations copyright © 2008 by Rob Bolster
All rights reserved. Published by Scholastic Inc.
SCHOLASTIC and associated logos are trademarks and/or registered trademarks of Scholastic Inc.

Lexile is a registered trademark of MetaMetrics, Inc.

12 11 10 9 8 7 6 5 4 3 2   8 9 10 11 12 13/0
Printed in the U.S.A.
First printing, September 2008

Start your brain.
Put on your running shoes.
Crawl, walk, trot, jog, run,
sprint, and zoom!
Let's compare speeds
of animals and machines!

SPEED measures how
fast you can travel
from one place to another.

How far can you travel
in one hour?
Speed is usually measured
in miles per hour (mph).

How far is school from your home?
How long does it take to get there?
How fast can you travel
from New York to California?

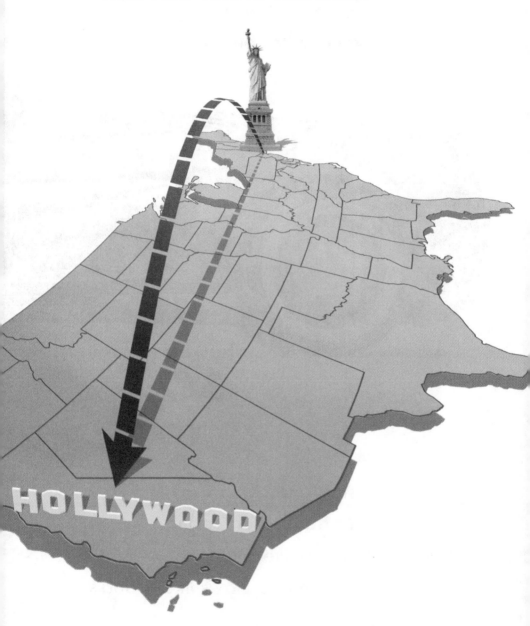

70 MPH

CHEETAH

A cheetah is the fastest mammal.
A cheetah runs in bursts,
up to seventy miles per hour.

It has to stop and catch
its breath after a short sprint.
A cheetah runs like a cat,
but it has teeth and claws like a dog's.

SPORTS CAR

A sports car can go more than
two hundred miles per hour.
That's faster than a cheetah!
A car does not have to stop
to catch its breath.
But it could run out of gas.

PIN-TAILED SWIFT

The pin-tailed swift is the fastest bird when flying across the sky.
It can fly one hundred miles per hour.
"Swift" is a good name for this bird!

WRIGHT BROTHERS' PLANE

Wilbur and Orville Wright built the first airplane more than a hundred years ago.

Their original flight lasted only twelve seconds.

They flew at a speed of seven miles per hour.

Birds were probably laughing at them!

Today, airplanes can fly much faster than birds.

PEREGRINE FALCON

A peregrine falcon is the fastest bird
when diving down.
This bird captures dinner by diving
onto smaller birds at high speeds.
It can swoop down through the air
at two hundred miles per hour.
The bird's hunting dive is called a stoop.

F-22 RAPTOR

Sound travels at seven hundred and
seventy miles per hour.
An F-22 Raptor can fly at a speed
of thirteen hundred miles per hour.
That's almost twice the speed of sound!
The pilot uses an onboard computer
to fly this fighter plane.
But a peregrine falcon dives down
all on its own.

11

HORSE

Animals vary their speeds as they move.
Horses walk at about three miles per hour.
They trot at five to ten miles per hour.
And they canter or lope at eleven
to seventeen miles per hour.
Their fastest speed is called galloping.
Horses gallop at thirty to fifty-five miles
per hour.

TRAIN

Years ago, trains were called "iron horses."
Today, high-speed and bullet trains
travel faster than one hundred miles
per hour.
Riding a horse might be more fun—
but a train ride is faster and
more comfortable.

FLY, DON'T WALK

DRAGONFLY

A dragonfly has six legs
but it cannot walk!
Yet it is the fastest insect.
The Australian dragonfly flies
at thirty-two miles per hour.
An ordinary housefly can fly
at about twenty-four miles per hour.

PITCHER THROWING BASEBALL

Some major league baseball players can throw a ball at one hundred miles per hour.

Most All-Star Little League pitchers throw a ball at around fifty miles per hour.

Watch out—don't hit the dragonfly!

70 MPH

SAILFISH

Swordfish, marlin, and sailfish
have long, swordlike noses.
They are known as billfish.
The fastest fish in the ocean is the sailfish.
It can swim seventy miles per hour.
The big, sail-shaped dorsal fin
allows it to make sharp turns.

JET SKI

Outboard motors have propellers.

Jet Skis have impellers.

An impeller is like a jet engine.

It sucks water in and blows it out the back.

A sailfish and a Jet Ski cruise along

at about the same speeds.

The Jet Ski can zoom across the water

as fast as fifty miles per hour.

But traveling fast on an ocean

or on a lake is dangerous.

So slow down, please!

12 MPH

BLACK MAMBA SNAKE

The black mamba lives in Africa.

It is the fastest snake in the world.

It can slither twelve miles per hour.

That's faster than a five-year-old child

can run!

These snakes can climb trees quickly, too.

Many people think the black mamba

is the most dangerous snake in the world.

MOWER

Have you seen someone drive
a lawn mower?
A sit-down lawn mower rolls and cuts
grass at about six miles per hour.
The fastest snake can move
twice as fast as that!

19

CREEPING ALONG

less than 1 MPH

SNAIL

A snail is a mollusk.

It has a shell on its body.

How do snails move?

They move very slowly.

They travel less than one mile per hour.

Snails are so slow that

we could measure their speed

in *inches* per hour!

SCHOOL BUS

A school bus travels much faster
than a snail.
A school bus driver usually drives
about thirty miles per hour.
Did you ever ride behind a bus
that made many stops to pick up kids?
You may feel as if you are traveling
at snail speed!

GREYHOUND

The fastest dog in the world
is the greyhound.
It can run forty-five miles per hour.
When running, greyhounds seem
to fly through the air.
You couldn't keep up with one
if you took it for a walk!

SOLAR-POWERED CAR

Some cars are powered by the sun.
College students have built one
that goes ninety miles per hour.
That speed is twice as fast as a greyhound's!
This kind of car will be able to go
even faster in the future.

FASTER THAN A BIKE

OLYMPIC SPRINTER

The fastest human being is an Olympic sprinter.
This athlete can run twenty-six miles per hour.
That fast speed is used in short races,
such as the one-hundred-yard dash.
A long-distance runner might travel
at about eleven miles per hour.

BICYCLE

A bicycle racer pedals a bike
at twenty-five miles per hour.
The bike goes up a steep hill
at three miles per hour.
It goes down a tall mountain even faster—
maybe ninety miles per hour.
The sprinter would start out faster
than the cyclist when on level ground.
But downhill, there is no contest.
A bicycle would zip by the sprinter!

COLUGO

A colugo is a mammal that lives
in the rain forest.
Its body looks like a furry blanket
with legs!
A colugo glides in the air from tree
to tree at about ten miles per hour.
This glider can travel more than
half the length of a football field at once!

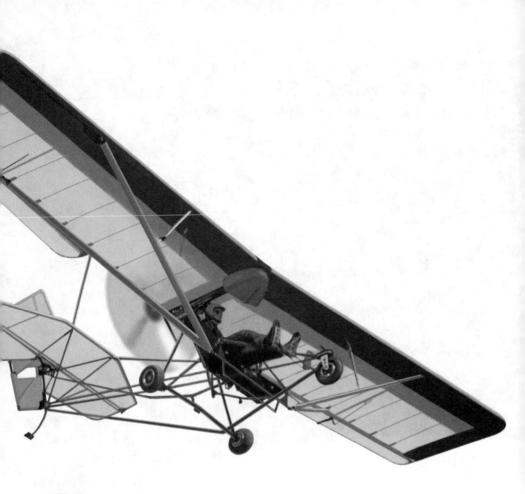

52 MPH

ULTRALIGHT

An ultralight is a small solo plane.
It is like a glider with a tiny motor.
Ultralights travel at about fifty miles
per hour.
A glider without a motor is no match
for a glider with one!

24,000 MPH

Apollo COMMAND AND SERVICE MODULES

What is the fastest any creature from Earth has ever gone? The *Apollo* astronauts who flew to the moon and back traveled at more than twenty-four thousand miles per hour.

Moon

SPACE TRAVEL

Someday astronauts will travel
to another planet.

Mars

A spaceship to Mars would travel
at more than one hundred thousand miles
per hour.

Are you ready to go?

BOOKS

Books don't move at all—
unless someone picks them up.
Books are stationary.
That means they stay in one place.
They go zero miles per hour.
Please pick one up and read!

GLOSSARY

bullet train: a very high-speed train in Japan

canines: dogs

capture: to catch someone or something

cruise: to move at a steady rate

dorsal: on the back of a body

mollusk: an animal with a soft body usually covered by a shell

motion: the act of moving; movement

ordinary: common or usual

original: the first of something

propeller: a shaft with turning blades that thrust water or air backward

rain forest: a tropical forest of trees with broad leaves that make a cover overhead

slither: to slide or glide easily

solar: coming from the sun

sprint: to run very fast for a short distance; a short fast race

stationary: not moving

vary: to change something; to change back and forth

INDEX